WILD ONES

POLAR BEARS

by JILL ANDERSON

NorthWord
Minnetonka, Minnesota

Brrr! Winter is very cold and snowy in the Arctic.

But this burly polar bear thinks the weather is just fine.

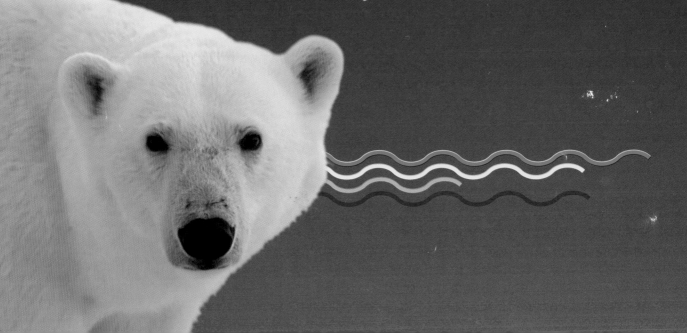

Polar bears have a
thick layer of fat called

blubber

to protect their insides,
and two layers of fur.

Their ears and tail are small and close to their bodies, so they won't freeze.

Check out those huge, furry paws!

The bumpy black pads
and sharp claws
help them to walk
on slippery ice.
They are also the
perfect tools for
hunting seals.

Polar bears are too big to chase down a meal. Usually they watch and wait—for hours or even days!—at a hole in the ice. When a seal comes up for air, it is in for a hairy, scary **surprise!**

Hunting seals is tricky. A polar bear needs years of practice, and a good teacher: its mother.

A mother polar bear gives birth to two babies, or cubs, at a time. It is the middle of winter, but the family stays **cozy** **and** **warm** in a den under the snow.

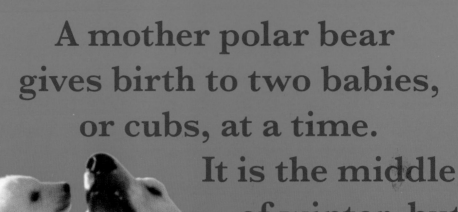

Each newborn cub is about the size of a loaf of bread.

The babies cannot see or hear,
and they have very little fur.

They snuggle with Mama
for warmth and milk.

In the spring, the family leaves the den behind.

z-z-z-z!!

Seals travel to cooler waters, so the bears follow. They take long rest breaks and short naps along the way.

During their
trip, the
mother may
have to fight
off male bears
twice her size.
But she is gentle
with her cubs.

She teaches her babies to hunt and helps them stay clean and warm.

The cubs watch
and learn until
they are nearly
two years old.

As the autumn days turn cooler, the cubs drift away from their mother.

She has taught them well, and they head off in search of their own icy adventures.

For my snuggly little cub, Leo

—J. A.

Composed in the United States of America
Designed by Lois A. Rainwater • Edited by Kristen McCurry

Text © 2007 by Jill Anderson

NORTHWORD
Books for Young Readers
11571 K-Tel Drive
Minnetonka, MN 55343
www.tnkidsbooks.com

Photographs © 2007 provided by:
Matthias Breiter/Minden Pictures: cover, pp. 13, 19; Suzi Eszterhas/Minden Pictures: endsheets;
Digital Vision/Punchstock: pp. 1, 18, 22-23; San Diego Zoo/Minden Pictures: pp. 2-3;
Shutterstock: back cover, pp. 4, 17, 20, 21, 24; Jim Brandenburg/Minden Pictures: p. 5;
Flip Nicklin/Minden Pictures: pp. 6, 8-9; Canstock Photo: p. 7;
Rinie Van Meurs/Foto Natura/Minden Pictures: pp. 10-11;
Mitsuaki Iwago/Minden Pictures: pp. 12, 14-15; Chris Schenk/Foto Natura/Minden Pictures: p. 16.

Library of Congress Cataloging-in-Publication Data

Polar bears / by Jill Anderson.
p. cm. -- (Wild ones)
ISBN 978-1-55971-974-2 (hc) -- ISBN 978-1-55971-975-9 (sc)
1. Polar bear--Juvenile literature. I. Title.

QL737.C27A525 2007

599.786--dc22   2006101498

Printed in Singapore
10 9 8 7 6 5 4 3 2 1

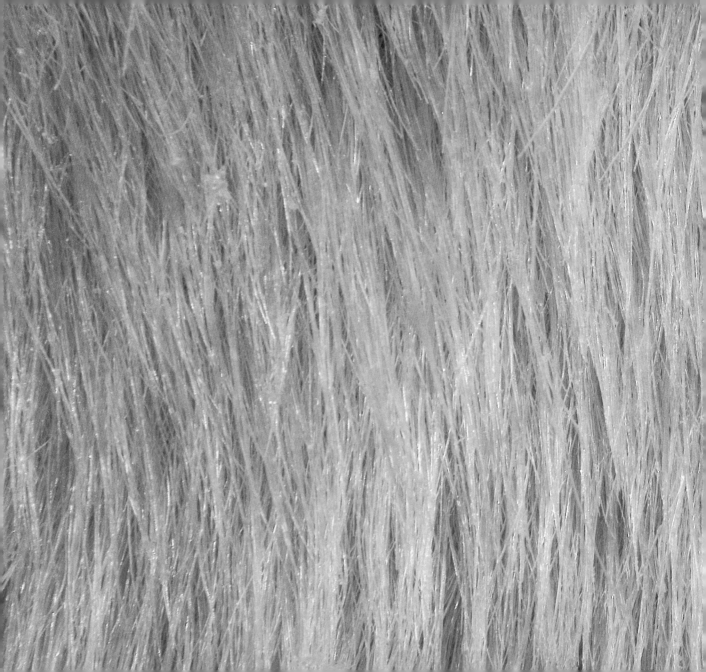